Gould, William
Business portraits
Kellogg's

BUSINESS PORTRAITS

KELLOGG'S®

Published by VGM Career Horizons,
a division of NTC Publishing Group
4255 West Touhy Avenue
Lincolnwood (Chicago),
Illinois 60646–1975,
U.S.A.

Library of Congress Cataloging-in-Publication Data
is available from the Library of Congress.

ISBN 0-8442-4780-4

Manufactured in Belgium by Proost
International Book Production.

BUSINESS PORTRAITS

KELLOGG'S®

WILLIAM GOULD

DISCARD

VGM Career Horizons
a division of *NTC Publishing Group*
Lincolnwood, Illinois USA

ACKNOWLEDGMENT

Our thanks to Kellogg Company for providing us with copies of its annual reports and historical publications from which we drew information to develop a profile of the Company. Editorial comments made and conclusions reached by the author about general business practices of international companies do not necessarily reflect the policies and practices of Kellogg Company.

Our thanks also to Cereal Partners Worldwide, General Mills, Nestlé, Quaker Oats, Ralston Foods, and Weetabix for providing us with information and permission to show their products.

CONTENTS

The adventure of business

Business often sounds difficult but its basic principles are simple, and it can be very exciting. The people involved in the creation and running of the businesses we examine in VGM'S BUSINESS PORTRAITS faced challenges and took risks that make some adventure stories seem dull.

What is a business?

If you sell your old computer to your friend for money you are making a business deal. Anyone who produces goods or services in return for money, or who works for an organization that does, is involved in business.

Businesses try to make profits. They try to sell things for more than the amount the things cost them to make. They usually invest part of the profit they make to produce and sell more of their product. If they have no money to invest, they may borrow it.

The language of business

Many of the technical terms that make the language of business sound complicated are explained on pages 46 and 47.

Business matters

Yellow panels throughout the book explain general business concepts. Blue panels tell you more about Kellogg.

■ People

■ Things

□ Money

▲ Businesses need people (human resources), things (physical resources) and money (capital).

▼ A business uses money to buy human and physical resources, and create a product or service which it sells for a profit.

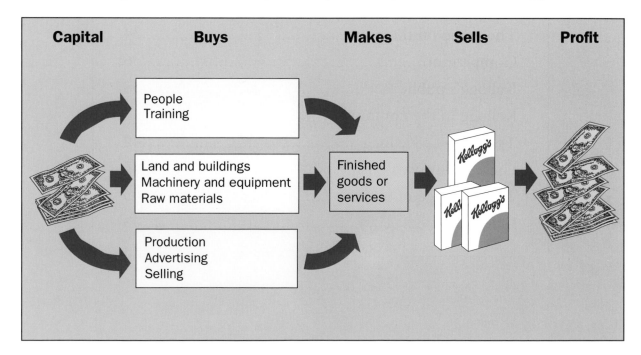

Capital	Buys	Makes	Sells	Profit

People
Training

Land and buildings
Machinery and equipment
Raw materials

Finished goods or services

Production
Advertising
Selling

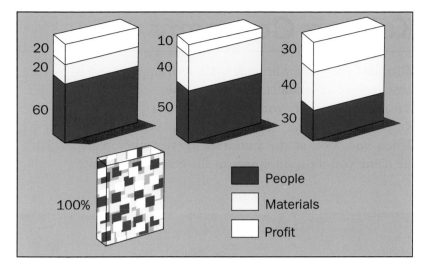

20
20
60

10
40
50

30
40
30

100%

People
Materials
Profit

◀ The purpose of a business is to make a profit. Profit is the amount of money earned from sales that remains after all the costs (for people and materials) are paid. If a box of Corn Flakes sells for one dollar and costs 80 cents to make and sell, the profit is 20 cents.

Kellogg's business

Each morning millions of children and adults in nearly 160 countries around the world wake up to an easily-prepared, tasty and nourishing breakfast of cereal made by Kellogg Company. Kellogg produces more than 40 different types of cereal products. The company also manufactures bagels and a range of convenience foods, from toaster pastries to frozen waffles. But cereals are what Kellogg is famous for.

Kellogg is also famous for its advertising and for promoting healthy eating. It supplies information and educational materials about nutrition for children and consumers of all ages.

▲ *Nutri-Grain* bars are made by Kellogg's Convenience Foods Division. Convenience foods are an expanding part of Kellogg's business.

◀ Kellogg's most famous product and the world's bestselling breakfast cereal is *Kellogg's Corn Flakes*.

Kellogg Company

What did you eat for breakfast this morning—eggs and bacon, toast, oatmeal, granola, muffins, fruit, cereal? If you had cereal, which did you choose—*Frosties, Coco Pops, Rice Krispies, Corn Flakes, Shredded Wheat, Sugar Puffs, Special K*? When you look at the hundreds of types of cereal available the name you most often see on the boxes is *Kellogg's*.

▲ Kellogg's main plant and the headquarters of its global operations is in Battle Creek, Michigan. The original plant was built in 1907.

King of Corn Flakes

At its global base in Battle Creek, Michigan, in the United States, Kellogg Company has been making ready-to-eat breakfast cereal foods since 1906. It was not the first company to market such products commercially, and it has always had considerable competition from other companies, but it remains the most successful. Kellogg sells its products all around the world and has sales worth more than $7 billion a year, of which four-fifths come from ready-to-eat cereals.

Kellogg owes its success to two major factors: its skill in producing healthy, high-quality, affordable foods that people enjoy and its skill in packaging, promoting, selling and advertising them.

KELLOGG FACTS

* The company has a 42 percent share of the world market in cereal foods.
* Its total assets amount to nearly $4.5 billion.
* Its headquarters are at One Kellogg Square, Battle Creek, Michigan.
* It has 34 manufacturing plants in 20 countries.
* It sells its products in nearly 160 countries.
* It directly employs nearly 14,500 people. Thousands more work for companies that supply Kellogg with raw materials and other services.
* It makes more than 40 different products.
* Ready-to-eat cereals represent 80 percent of Kellogg's business.
* Twelve of the 15 best-selling cereals in the world are made by Kellogg.

▲ Around the world some 200 million people already start the day with a bowl of *Kellogg's* cereal. But there is still a fast-growing market, especially in Asia.

▼ Nutrition and health have always been genuine concerns of Kellogg.

* The Irish eat more cereal than anyone else in the world. Consumption of cereal in Ireland stands at more than 17 pounds per person per year. Yet Kellogg's market continues to expand there.
* In 1906, at the end of its first year of trading, Kellogg was shipping nearly 3,000 cases of *Kellogg's Corn Flakes* a day. By 1920, the figure was 24,000. Today daily shipments are numbered in millions.

Eating for health

Health and nutrition have always been vital to Kellogg. The company's founder, Will Keith Kellogg, was convinced of their importance as a result of his years working at the Battle Creek Sanitarium, the health establishment where cereal foods first became popular and where flaked grains were first developed. Throughout its existence, the company has promoted nutrition and particularly the importance of breakfast to health. It has pioneered accurate and honest package labeling, and its educational materials have won awards. Kellogg finances its health promotion activities from its large profits. Of course, telling people about the nutritional advantages of healthy eating helps the company to sell more cereal.

Will Keith Kellogg (1860-1951) was born in Battle Creek. He left school at 14 and went to work as a salesman for his father's broom factory. In his late teens, W.K. spent a year in Texas, where he became superintendent of another broom factory. He moved back to Michigan in 1879 and, after taking a short business management course, spent the next 25 years working for his brother Dr. John Harvey Kellogg at the Battle Creek Sanitarium. In 1906, W.K. set up his own company to sell cereal products he had developed. This became the Kellogg Company in 1922. W.K. devoted his life to the business, often at the expense of his family. He neither smoked nor drank and had little time for other pleasures. He was a strict boss and father but a kind, fair man at heart. In 1930, he set up the W. K. Kellogg Foundation. He died at the age of 91.

The birth of Corn Flakes

The founder of Kellogg Company, Will Keith Kellogg (or W.K., as he was known), once said that he was afraid he would always be broke. At school his teachers regarded him as a slow learner, and he was 20 years old before he discovered that he was not slow at all—he just had poor eyesight. By then he had been at work on and off for six years.

In 1880, W.K. went to work for his older brother Dr. John Harvey Kellogg at the Battle Creek Sanitarium, or "San." He was employed as a bookkeeper but soon found that he was expected to carry out virtually every other non-medical task, too. One job was helping J.H. in his search for tasty nutritious foods for the patients. With and without his brother, he carried out kitchen experiments, often working late into the night.

How Corn Flakes began

In 1894, J.H. Kellogg heard about Shredded Wheat, a ready-to-eat cereal invented by Henry Perky of Denver, Colorado. Instantly J.H. thought he could do better, and he and W.K. set about inventing their own wheat-based food. One day, while preparing to pass some cooked wheat through rollers,

they were called away on other business. Left unattended for two days, the wheat almost dried out, but the brothers decided to use it anyway to see what would happen. What came out from the rollers was not the long, flat sheets of dough they had expected, but thin flakes. Each wheat kernel had been flattened into a small sliver of grain. The wheat flakes, when toasted, tasted crisp and light. The Kellogg brothers had discovered a new breakfast food by accident.

A business opportunity

The flaked grains and other foods devised by the brothers proved very popular with the clients of the San. They liked them so much that they wanted to continue eating them even after they had finished their treatment and gone home. To satisfy their demand, J.H. Kellogg set up a small business to produce and sell the cereal by mail order. He called the business the Sanitas Food Company and gave W.K. the job of running it. Sanitas sold to a very restricted market. Seeing how popular the foods were becoming, W.K. realized that selling to a wider market—the general public—would make the business much more profitable. Sold as ready-to-eat health foods for all, rather than for the few, Corn Flakes would make a fortune. "I'm not interested in selling Corn Flakes by mail," he once said, "I want to sell them by the carload."

▲ Granose Flakes were sold as a health food to the clients of the Sanitarium.

THE SAN

Dr. John Harvey Kellogg (1852-1943) was physician-in-chief of the Battle Creek Sanitarium from 1876 to 1943. The San was a non-profit institution owned by the Seventh-Day Adventists, a strict religious sect to which the Kellogg family belonged. A cross between a hospital and health farm, the San promoted health reforms and clean living, and gained an international reputation. Dr. Kellogg evolved a theory called "biologic living": it emphasized fresh air, proper rest, exercise and a strict, calorie-controlled diet of natural foods; regular bowel movements; and a ban on caffeine, meat, tobacco and sex.

◀ An artist's impression of the moment when the Kellogg brothers discovered the technique for making wheat flakes.

BUSINESS MATTERS: MASS MARKET

Some companies make a profit by selling high-quality products for high prices to a small number of people who can afford them. Other companies sell products that are attractive enough and cheap enough to appeal to ordinary people—the mass market. W.K. knew that selling to the masses was the key to business success.

The business begins

W.K. and J.H. Kellogg did not always work well together. Though he did not publicly complain, W.K. was paid less and given less recognition than he deserved. As manager of Sanitas Foods, W.K. tried to expand the business, but his brother opposed him. Dr. Kellogg was not good with money and kept the businesses small, for fear that larger concerns might take them over. As a doctor he was also opposed to advertising on professional and ethical grounds.

Eventually, in mid-1901, W.K. gave up working for J.H. at the San in order to strike out on his own. But a disastrous fire at the San in February of 1902 disrupted his plans for a new company, and W.K. spent the next two and a half years helping his brother get back on his feet.

▲ The Battle Creek Sanitarium as it was in 1897. Here John Kellogg invented exercise machines, sun lamps, water treatments, a form of aerobics and a host of vegetarian foods, including peanut butter.

Promoting Corn Flakes and W.K.

W.K. continued to manage Sanitas, where he was responsible to a board of directors, rather than just his brother. He focused his attention more and more on promoting and improving Corn Flakes. Encouraged by his friend and business adviser, Arch Shaw, he made the cereals more appealing by adding malt and cane sugar to them (the use of sugar was much against J.H.'s policy). From 1901, Sanitas employed an advertising

agency to promote Corn Flakes as a nutritious, tasty morning meal for everyone.

In 1905, W.K. Kellogg won the confidence of Charles D. Bolin, an insurance man from St. Louis, Missouri, who was a patient at the San. Together they planned to launch a new company to manufacture Corn Flakes. Bolin persuaded some of his friends in the St. Louis business community to buy shares in the company and provide the financial capital. Six months later, on February 19, 1906, after hard and bitter legal and financial bargaining with J.H. over the rights to Corn Flake manufacture, W.K.'s Battle Creek Toasted Corn Flake Company was incorporated.

BUSINESS MATTERS: ENTREPRENEURS

Business people are always looking for good ideas to fill gaps in the market, products and services that people would want if they were available. An entrepreneur is a business owner or manager who recognizes and exploits new opportunities and is prepared to take a risk to do so. Entrepreneurs often invest in untried projects in the hope of making a large profit before anyone else gets a chance. W.K. had the entrepreneurial spirit and good business sense.

BREAKFAST'S READY

Cereals, rice and potatoes are the world's staple diets. All three have to be cooked before they can be digested, and cooking takes time. Once people ate large breakfasts of cooked cereals and bread— and meat and eggs if they could afford them. Most ordinary people did hard physical work on the land, so they needed plenty of food in the morning. Gradually more people lived in towns and worked in offices and factories. With everyone hurrying to work or school, there was no time to cook hot cereal. Ready-to-eat cereals that needed only the addition of cold milk were great time-savers and busy people flocked to buy them. Breakfast took no time at all to prepare and serve.

Success!

In 1906, W.K. wrote to Arch Shaw: "I sort of feel it in my bones that we are now preparing for a campaign on a food that will eventually prove to be the leading cereal of the United States, if not the world." They were prophetic words: at its first factory, an inadequate but cheap property in Bartlett Street, Battle Creek, the company was turning out 33 cases of *Kellogg's Toasted Corn Flakes* a day in the spring of 1906. By the end of the year that figure had leapt to nearly 3,000.

BATTLE CREEK BOOM

W.K. Kellogg was not alone in seeing the profitable possibilities of Corn Flakes and other cereals. Other enterprising people realized them too. By 1904, some 42 factories had sprung up in the Battle Creek area, copying Sanitas products and selling them under different names. Many disappeared as quickly as they had appeared. But the brief boom in health foods brought Battle Creek a lasting reputation as the health-food capital of the world.

▲ You may need a magnifying glass to read the words on this cartoon from the Chicago Tribune which wittily depicts the craziness of the Battle Creek health-food boom.

Growth

W.K. was right. The nutty malt flavor of Corn Flakes appealed to all consumers, not just those who were ill. Kellogg and Shaw also proved to have a gift for marketing. *Kellogg's Toasted Corn Flakes* came in easy-to-recognize boxes bearing W.K.'s signature and the warning "None genuine without this signature." Kellogg's advertising and salesmanship were outstanding and sales continued to grow.

Because of its rapid growth, the young company had little

money to spare. It used every cent it had to buy equipment and raw materials so that it could satisfy the demand created by its advertising, which was itself a major expense.

Disaster overcome

The company's factory was little more than a shack, and on July 4, 1907—Independence Day—it burned down. Most of the equipment was wrecked. Production had to be switched hurriedly to a tiny support factory, and the company fell behind in filling orders.

The disaster coincided with a decline in the Battle Creek food boom. There were too many food companies chasing too few consumers. Local banks were no longer willing to lend money to food companies and refused to help W.K. finance a new factory. In the end, he found a small Chicago bank prepared to take a chance on him, and five months later his new custom-built, fireproof factory was in operation.

Continuing growth

When he opened his new plant in 1907, W.K. said: "Now we can turn out 4,200 cases a day, and that's all the business I ever want." Production at the factory soon overtook that figure. Outstanding orders were filled and the bank loan was paid off. In 1909, when the company formally changed its name to the Kellogg Toasted Corn Flake Company, it sold over a million cases of *Kellogg's Toasted Corn Flakes.*

▲ This early box of Toasted Corn Flakes proclaims the Sanitas name and W.K.'s signature so that loyal Sanitarium customers will know that the product is genuine.

▲ W.K. made several sales trips. He once personally sold a trainload of *Kellogg's Toasted Corn Flakes* to one single food wholesaler, and was quick to advertise the fact.

BUSINESS MATTERS: CAPITAL AND INVESTMENT

People go into business to make money. But to get a company going, you need capital—money with which to buy equipment and factory space. Because W.K. did not have enough money of his own, he had to borrow what he needed. He might have borrowed from a bank, but instead borrowed from the St. Louis investors who bought stock to the value of $35,000. It was money well spent. Money borrowed from a bank has to be repaid over time with interest (the cost of borrowing the money). Investors who buy stock (a block of shares) in a company are entitled to a share of the company's profits. If the company does well, they make money. If the business does not make money, debts cannot be repaid, and the investors may lose their money.

Kellogg's advertising

Although W.K. was a cautious man, he was fearless when it came to advertising, calmly allocating it the major part of the company's capital. He and Arch Shaw, who handled the advertising from Chicago, created campaigns that have become part of business legend.

Creating a demand

In order to create a demand for his product, W.K. made the public aware of *Kellogg's Corn Flakes* even before they could buy them in the food stores. The most influential magazine of the time was *Ladies' Home Journal*. In May 1906, the company

took a full-page advertisement in the magazine. The ad, in the form of a letter, said that the Toasted Corn Flake Company was snowed under with orders and could not fill any new ones until July. This gave the impression that the product was so good that people could not get enough of it. This was not true as production had scarcely begun, but it did the trick. People felt a desperate need for *Kellogg's Corn Flakes*. Another advertisement that stimulated demand showed a woman winking and the slogan "Give the grocer a wink and see what you'll get." It was a bold ad for the time.

▼ *Tony the Tiger* is now so well known that children can recognize him by a solitary tail or paw. In the early days, Kellogg's ads targeted the housewife with images of wholesome female role models.

TM

◀ In 1912, Kellogg erected the largest electric sign then known on a roof in Times Square, New York. It was 50 feet high and 106 feet wide.

Advertising today

Kellogg was among the first to use full color in its ads. *The Sweetheart of the Corn* ads, featuring a succession of pretty country girls, gave the product a wholesome but alluring image that endures today. Today, in the countries where it operates, Kellogg's own marketing and design departments work with outside advertising agencies, such as J. Walter Thompson and Leo Burnett, to produce local advertising campaigns. In the United States, for example, Kellogg has sponsored many popular radio and television programs over the years. Kellogg spends more than $250 million a year on advertising.

TM

▲ Each of Kellogg's main brands is embodied by a character. *Tony the Tiger* gives a fun feeling to *Frosties. Cornelius* the perky *Corn Flake* rooster says rise and shine! It's breakfast time!

◀ *Snap! Crackle! Pop!* are the names of the lively characters who advertise *Rice Krispies*, the world's only talking cereal.

TM

17

▲ Intrigued to find the meaning of K.T.C., women winked at the grocer and got a free sample of *Kellogg's Toasted Corn Flakes*.

Promotion and sales

Wherever W.K. traveled in the United States, he expected to see his products. His salesmen (in those days no women were employed in selling) knew that their jobs depended on their performance. Everyone likes to have something for nothing, and W.K. was eager that people should taste his product and get to know the look of it, so that they would demand his brand, complete with signature, and no other. He believed that it was best to reach people in their own homes.

Teams of "samplers" went from door to door delivering free sample boxes of *Corn Flakes* to consumers at home. Kellogg also packed cartons for store delivery into cases that were slightly bigger than necessary so that there would be room for samples that grocers could pass on to consumers.

Another method the company used to create an interest in the product before it was available, was to employ people to

BUSINESS MATTERS: MARKETING

Marketing is the whole process by which goods get from producers to buyers. Marketing involves:
   market research—seeing who wants what kind of product at what price
   product development—making the product right for its market
   distribution—getting goods from the producers to the retail customers
   pricing—setting the right price, one that will please customers, beat competition and still leave a profit
   promotion—dressing the product, advertising, nationally, locally and at the place of sale, selling, organizing promotions and after sales service.

A GIFT FOR MARKETING

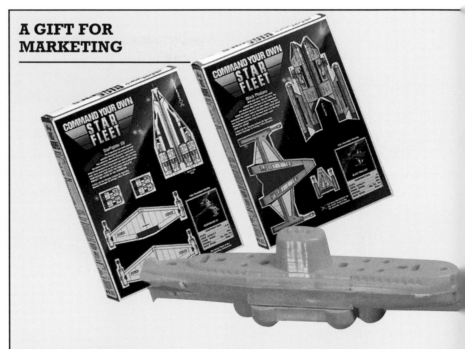

Kellogg's marketing departments devised many memorable promotional gifts. The first, in 1910, was a children's cartoon book, called the *Funny Jungleland Moving Picture Book.* One

packet insert that delighted children in the late 1950s was an "atomic submarine." This simple scientific device was powered by baking soda and could dive and resurface in the bath. Even

visit all the stores in an area and ask for *Corn Flakes*. When the first consignments became available, the storekeepers snapped them up to satisfy the demand that Kellogg itself had created.

Premiums

Once consumers are habitually buying your product, you need to find ways of keeping them loyal. A box of breakfast cereal is a simple item, its contents the same today as they were yesterday. To give customers added value and an extra incentive to buy, Kellogg made the boxes desirable in themselves and gave away collectible promotional items inside or alongside them. These free gifts are called premiums and Kellogg was among the first to use them. Over the years they have taken many forms, from plastic toys and picture cards sealed inside the boxes to puzzles, games and cutouts printed on the back of them. Kellogg also helped to pioneer the selling of promotional items.

▲ House-to-house sampling began in 1903. Ads like this one got people expectantly talking about the product.

the navy tested it, taking it to a depth of nearly 42 feet. Another simple gift that created a run on *Corn Flakes* was the Dood-L-oon, a balloon you could draw on before blowing it up to produce weirdly distorted shapes. These cheap items, designed to boost sales and then be thrown away, are today eagerly sought by collectors willing to pay high prices.

SPECIAL PROMOTIONS

Today virtually every product in food stores is at some time accompanied by a special promotion. Shoppers collect box tops to get a reduction in the price of the next box, or to send off as part payment for some desirable item, or to qualify for a competition. One of Kellogg's early promotions advertised a set of three silver-plated spoons in return for cash and box tops. The great success of the promotion took Kellogg by surprise, and the silver-spoon manufacturer almost collapsed under the huge volume of orders for the spoons.

All businesses rely on an uninterrupted supply of raw materials that comply with their quality standards. When a business is small, it is unable to buy at the best prices and may be at the mercy of its suppliers. Large companies can buy at better prices. Some own or control their suppliers to ensure that they are never let down. The quality, price and supply of Kellogg's most important materials—cereal crops, paper and sugar—are all subject to variable weather and market conditions.

▼ *Corn Flakes* are made from corn not wheat (shown here). Wheat is used to make many other cereals, including *All-Bran*.

From cornfield to consumer

The complex process of bringing you a bowl of *Kellogg's Corn Flakes* begins with the harvesting of sun-ripened corn by large combine-harvesters. The grain is then transported by road, rail or sea to any of 34 Kellogg plants in 20 countries world-wide. The grain is stored temporarily in huge silos. In the next stage, the grain is milled to remove unwanted parts of the corn, leaving only the "grits"—the sweet heart of the corn!

The grits are blended with sugar, malt and salt and then cooked under steam pressure. The cooked corn, still steaming, is partly dried for several hours in a current of purified hot air. It is tempered and caramelized and eventually passed between very heavy flaking rollers. The resulting flakes are toasted in rotary ovens and extra nutrients are added to them. Then they flow by gravity into filling machines, from which they are

dispensed with precision into individual inner liners. The filled and sealed liners pass along conveyors to be packed into cartons. The cartons, made up into cases, are sent to warehouses and from there are loaded on to trucks or trains and dispatched to retailers.

Quality assured

At every stage of the manufacturing process, the standard of every type of cereal is rigorously checked. Trained employees regularly test all the materials that go into the making of each cereal product. Finished products are spot-checked and their contents analyzed to make sure that the balance of ingredients is right.

Modern technology has produced machines that provide reliable analysis of Kellogg's products. In addition, experienced tasters meet regularly to compare all the cereals being made. Their job is to confirm that high standards are being maintained.

◀ After flavoring, cooking and drying, the corn mixture is flaked, toasted and inspected, before being packed and shipped.

▲ *Kellogg's Rice Krispies* follow much the same process. The boxes travel by conveyor belts to be automatically packed into cases and containers.

New products

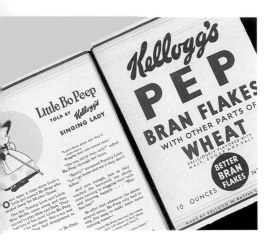

▲ Not all Kellogg's brands have been a success. Despite the help of Little Bo Peep, *Pep* never took off, though *Kellogg's Bran Flakes* themselves are among Kellogg's ten top brands.

For nine years after its foundation, W.K.'s company sold nothing but *Kellogg's Corn Flakes*. It was hugely successful, but like all firms, Kellogg had to grow. Customers feel loyal to the brands they know, but they also like a choice. To avoid its customers going to competitors for a change, Kellogg had to create new products and find new markets.

It opened its first plant outside the United States in 1914 (with a factory in London, Ontario, Canada). The first new product came in 1915 with the introduction of 40% Bran. *All-Bran* came a year later. By 1920, the company's output was 24,000 cases a day.

In 1922, the company shortened its name to Kellogg Company. In 1928 it began marketing *Kellogg's Rice Krispies*. Over the years, hosts of other products have been added, especially since the end of World War II, when people in developed countries began to be more prosperous.

A changing world

In most western countries, people now have more money and

KELLOGG'S PRODUCTS

Kellogg's Corn Flakes
All-Bran
Rice Krispies
Frosties
Ricicles
Coco Pops
Nut & Honey Crunch
Honey Smacks
Kellogg's Bran Flakes (or
   Complete Bran Flakes)
Special K
Kellogg's Sultana Bran
Bran Buds
Country Store
Kellogg's Low Fat Granola
Kellogg's Fruit 'n Fibre
Start
Kellogg's Raisin Bran
Frosted Mini-Wheats
Froot Loops

more leisure time than they did 50 years ago. The pace of life has also quickened, with even fewer people having the time or desire to cook breakfast. More women, including mothers, go out to work. People need products that will be fast to serve and eat, satisfy a continuous need for variety, and be healthy.

In 1955, the company launched *Special K*, a malt-flavored cereal made of rice and whole wheat flakes that was the first low-calorie high-protein breakfast food on the market. During the 1960s, the company introduced its first grain-based non-cereal product, fruit-filled pastries called *Pop-Tarts* that consumers could pop into the toaster. In 1976, it produced its first muesli-type cereal, *Country Store*. In 1981, it launched *Nutri-Grain*, a high-fiber, low-calorie cereal with no added sugar.

Change of size

Another way in which Kellogg has reacted to change is in the size of packaging. Not everyone in a family enjoys the same cereal. So in the late 1950s Kellogg introduced the popular *Variety* packs. In addition, institutional-size boxes have been introduced for hotels, restaurants, hospitals, and other organizations and businesses that like to buy in bulk.

Smacks
Apple Jacks
Apfel Zimt Loops (Germany)
Crackles (France)
Pop-Tarts
Eggo waffles
Sustain
Nutri-Grain
Mini-Wheats
Healthy Choice
Rice Krispies Treats
Corn Pops
Choco Krispis
Basmati Flakes (India)
Temptations
Pop-Tarts Crunch

◄ These are just some of Kellogg's products. *Healthy Choice*® is licensed from Con Agra. All the other products are brand names of Kellogg Company.

Branching out

When a market is shrinking—for instance when fewer babies are being born—many companies grow by turning to another type of product, one that may or may not be related to their core products. For a time, in the 1970s and 1980s, Kellogg sought to expand its market by acquiring companies such as Whitney's Foods, a yogurt manufacturer, Fearn International Inc., producers of food for the catering trade, Salada Foods Inc., tea packagers, and Mrs. Smith's Frozen Foods, makers of a wide range of frozen convenience foods from pies to soups. Among the most popular lines were *Eggo* waffles. Kellogg also bought companies in other parts of the world, including a snack-food business in Argentina.

The world economy was good and Kellogg's profits grew. But then, in the late 1980s, there was a recession and business

▲ **Mexican products**

▲ **Kellogg Guatemala**

◀ About 20 percent of Kellogg's turnover comes from convenience foods. As well as an increased assortment of breakfast foods, the company hopes to create more new products with all day appeal.

BUSINESS MATTERS: DIVERSIFICATION

There is a limit to the amount anyone can sell of a single product. Businesses need to expand and often they do so by creating new products or buying other companies to acquire ready-made new products. The widening of a range of business activities is called diversification. Having a range of products helps to spread risk. If one product is doing badly, another may be doing well. In a wet summer, ice cream might sell slowly, umbrellas fast. One danger of diversification is that buying into different businesses is expensive. You might have to borrow the money and get into debt, and the new product might not be successful. When times are hard, you might be forced to sell off one of your businesses and lose money on the sale.

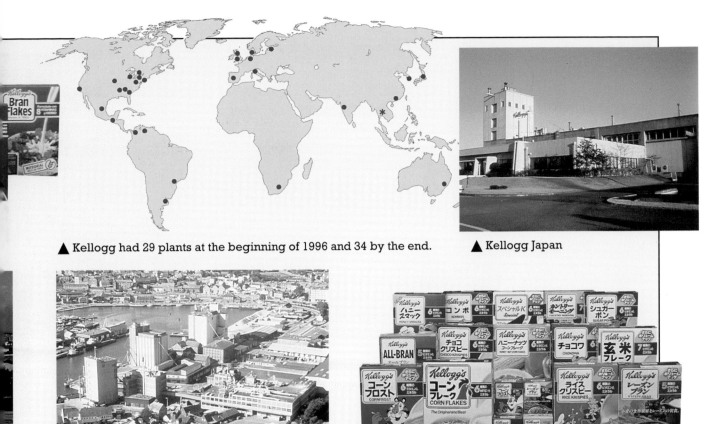

▲ Kellogg had 29 plants at the beginning of 1996 and 34 by the end.

▲ Kellogg Japan

▲ Kellogg Denmark

▲ Japanese products

became tougher for everyone. The price of Kellogg's stocks dropped. Kellogg returned to concentrating mostly on what it does best—making cereals and convenience foods. It sold off the Argentine snack-food business in 1993 and Mrs. Smith's in 1994. A new Convenience Foods division set up in 1993 continues to make and sell *Eggo* waffles and *Pop-Tarts*. In 1996 Kellogg acquired Lender's Bagel Bakery.

Going global

As well as creating new products, Kellogg has been successful in reaching new markets, and in changing people's eating habits. In many developing countries breakfast has traditionally consisted of bread or rice. As these countries have grown more prosperous, Kellogg has expanded into them, opening up new areas of operation in Asia (especially China and India) and Eastern Europe. In each area Kellogg products have quickly become popular.

BUSINESS MATTERS: RECESSION AND BOOM

Recession is a period during which a nation's business declines. Fewer goods are bought and sold. As a result there are fewer jobs and people have less to spend, so even fewer goods are sold. Businesses use any means they can to increase their sales. If they cannot they may go bankrupt. During boom times, people have more money to spend. Businesses thrive and unemployment falls.

The science of breakfast

▲ Kellogg advertised the benefits to health of *All-Bran* (shown here) and other high-fiber cereals long before governments and health authorities began to recommend them.

▶ A chemist, a product improvement manager and a product development technologist share their ideas. Expertise in nutrition, quality, marketing and technology are all necessary for the creation of new and improved products.

WHAT IS A HEALTHY BREAKFAST?

Nutritionists agree it is healthy to include a high proportion of cereal-based foods in the daily diet of children and adults. The U.S. Department of Agriculture recommends 6-11 servings per day of bread, pasta or cereals. It is one of 122 countries whose governments and health organizations have made such recommendations. Doctors also believe that wheat-bran fiber in a low-fat high-fiber diet may help lower the risk of breast and colon cancer.

Every year Kellogg introduces new products to its line and drops less popular ones. The company also carries out scientific studies to improve the foods it already produces—studies to make its *Rice Krispies* crispier, its *Corn Pops* tastier, and to ensure that all its products are safe, healthy and of a consistent high quality. It fortifies most of its products with added vitamins and minerals.

Kellogg currently spends more than $70 million a year on research and development, striving to introduce new technologies that will cut costs and help create ever more popular products. A new $75-million research and development facility is due to open at Battle Creek in 1997. Its other factories throughout the world also have departments engaged in research and development to suit their local markets.

Market research

In the old days at the San, W.K. was able to observe exactly how well the clients liked new foods. Gauging the tastes of millions of consumers around the world is not so simple, and launching a new product is expensive. To avoid making costly mistakes, Kellogg spends time and money on product testing and market research. Small focus groups of consumers are asked to tell Kellogg what they want from their cereal and are invited to try out the new products. The products are then tested in small target areas with free samples, local advertising

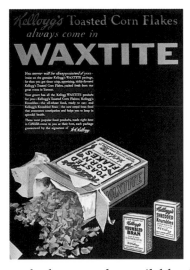

◀ To remain at their best, cereals need to be kept dry. Paraffin-waxed paper liners that kept moisture out were a tremendous innovation. Today the liners are made of plastic.

and the cereals available in stores. The response can be measured and translated into a probable national response.

▲ Products are continuously tested for freshness, taste and texture and routinely analyzed to make sure that the ingredients printed on the box are present in the quantities stated.

Packaging freshness and information

Fresh foods have a shelf life. Foods sealed against the air stay fresher longer. Kellogg's introduced patented Waxtite paper in 1914. The lining bags, which could be resealed inside the cardboard boxes, kept the cereals fresh in the stores and in the kitchen cupboard. The liners have continued to be improved over the years. Recently bag-free boxes have been introduced.

Today food manufacturers are obliged to label their products to state what they contain. But Kellogg started labeling their boxes long ago. Today the nutrition information includes the total energy in calories, together with the amounts of protein, carbohydrate (sugars and starch), fat, fiber, vitamins, and minerals. Boxes also have a "best-by" date.

FOLIC ACID

Folic acid is an important B-vitamin. Deficiency of it in the diet of pregnant women is thought to be associated with birth defects. In 1996, Kellogg and the March of Dimes organization jointly publicized the importance of folic acid during and prior to pregnancy. Kellogg's cereals are of course enriched with folic acid.

◀ Kellogg spells out its key ingredients so that health-conscious consumers can see at a glance whether the product contains what they do or don't want to eat.

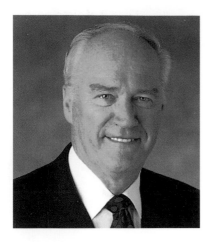

▲ Chief executive officer and chairman of the board Arnold G. Langbo.

How Kellogg manages

Kellogg Company is a public company quoted on the New York Stock Exchange. It is owned by its stockholders. The board of directors runs the company for the stockholders and is answerable to them. The directors must account for their actions to the stockholders at an annual general meeting and must publish the company's results in an annual report. The stockholders have a right to vote on decisions that affect the company as a whole but they leave the day-to-day running of the company to the board of directors.

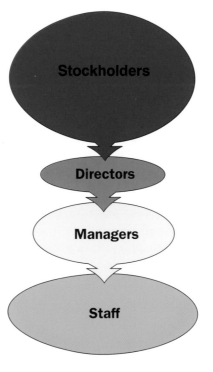

◀ A public company like Kellogg is owned by its stockholders. The board of directors is answerable to them. The management and staff are answerable to the board. In Kellogg's case, many of the staff are also stockholders.

<table>
<tr><td>Stockholders</td></tr>
<tr><td>Directors</td></tr>
<tr><td>Managers</td></tr>
<tr><td>Staff</td></tr>
</table>

BUSINESS MATTERS: MANAGEMENT

At every level of a company, it is important for people to work as efficiently as possible. Managers have the job of seeing that they do. They have the task of ensuring that their staff are able to do their work efficiently, cost-effectively and on time. They must make sure that employees are confident and happy in their work and feel well rewarded and eager for promotion. No matter how good the workers are, they cannot perform well with a poor management that lacks direction and drive, or fails to understand the workers' problems.

The board of directors

Kellogg Company's board of directors currently has 12 members. Some of these are executive directors who work full time for Kellogg. The others are non-executive directors who do not work for the company. They are chosen for their business experience in other industries. They help the other directors by giving unbiased advice and resolving problems over company policy or conduct.

The chairman of the board supervises its meetings and ensures that its decisions are carried out by the company. Kellogg's current chairman and chief executive is Arnold G. Langbo.

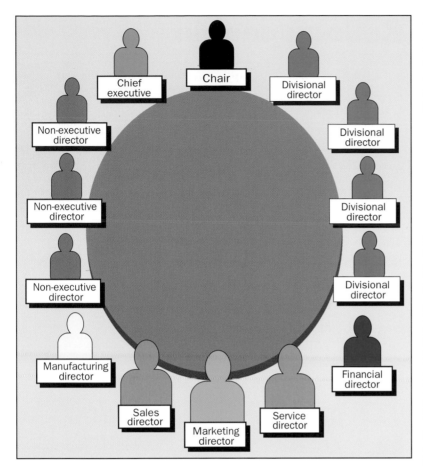

Labels in figure: Chief executive · Chair · Divisional director · Divisional director · Divisional director · Non-executive director · Divisional director · Non-executive director · Divisional director · Non-executive director · Financial director · Manufacturing director · Sales director · Marketing director · Service director

Corporate officers

The chairman delegates responsibility to other directors who control various divisions of the company. These directors are called corporate officers, executive presidents or vice presidents. They include a chief financial officer, a treasurer, a company secretary, a lawyer, and a large number of other officers, many of whom serve on various subcommittees of the board. Kellogg currently has seven such subcommittees but the number is not fixed. All companies change their structure from time to time as they see possibilities for improvement.

Global management

With modern communication and ease of movement around the world, Kellogg has been able to globalize its structure. Many of its managers and engineers are international, trained to operate anywhere in the world. Knowledge and experience gained in one part of Kellogg's world can instantly benefit another part as people travel from country to country.

BUSINESS MATTERS: LABOR RELATIONS

The employees of a large company often feel that they need to belong to an organization that represents their interests in discussions with the company's management. Such an organization is called a trade union. The elected officers of the union meet with the management to negotiate rates of pay, working hours, and other conditions of employment. Relations between employers and unions have not always been friendly. Some big companies in the United States will not employ union members, but Kellogg does employ union labor in some departments. There have been disputes in the past, but generally management and unions work well together.

Kellogg people

In 1906, W.K. Kellogg's company had 25 employees. Today Kellogg has 14,500 throughout the world. Kellogg's understands that its most important asset is its people. It is an equal opportunity employer and pledges itself to respect the cultural diversity of its people. Its aim is to attract, select and retain top-quality people. The company provides training, development and growth opportunities, giving workers high levels of responsibility for on-the-spot decision making. This is not simply to make sure that they can do their jobs efficiently but also to ensure that they know what Kellogg's policies and goals are and will play their part effectively in working towards them.

▲ Kellogg employees take pride in their work and show it off to their visitors.

▶ It is 1914 and Kellogg's Battle Creek employees assemble in their Sunday best for the firm's annual picnic. The event allowed a brief flurry of relaxed informality.

BUSINESS MATTERS: HUMAN RESOURCES

At one time, it took thousands of people to do unskilled or manual jobs. Now these jobs are done by machines controlled by computers. There is less demand for unskilled workers but more for people with talents and skills—creative people full of ideas, persuasive salespeople, and people who are good at being leaders. That is why it is good for people looking for jobs to train and realize their full potential.

Shared achievements and rewards

As in many successful business organizations, the workers at Kellogg are encouraged to believe strongly in the products they help to make and sell and to be loyal to their company. Employees are able to become stockholders in the company and more than 12,000 employees own Kellogg's stock. Where possible the company promotes people from within, recognizing achievements and rewarding performance. The aim is to create an environment in which people share the same values, can communicate openly and benefit from each other's experience.

Kellogg builds its employees' collective pride in their work by means of its Achievement Award or President's Cup. Any organization within its global network may win either of these awards for outstanding productivity or sales results. The company may also make special awards to outstanding or long-serving individual employees.

Fit for work and play

Many of Kellogg's factories have sports clubs and recreational facilities. The company promotes the use of these facilities as a means of helping employees relax during lunch breaks or non-working hours. It even sponsors company teams in sports such as baseball and soccer. A regular newsletter, *The Kellogg News,* keeps employees up to date with business matters and with the social life of the company.

▲ The winners celebrate and hold up their trophy. Friendly rivalry with other teams keeps people on their toes and gives winners a sense of achievement.

CAREERS AT KELLOGG

The people who work directly for Kellogg in Battle Creek and elsewhere do a large number of different jobs. There are plant workers who operate the equipment used in preparing the products; packers and shippers who prepare the products for transportation to retail outlets; and food technologists who regularly

and rigorously check product quality and research new lines. There are grain buyers and sales staff. There are accountants and accounts clerks, publicity and public relations staff, marketing and design staff, security personnel, legal staff and administrators.

In addition to its directly employed work force, Kellogg employs the services of law firms, advertising agencies and a host of smaller concerns.

Money matters

A company makes its money from the sale of its products or services. This is called income or revenue. At the same time as it is making money by selling products, it is spending money in manufacturing them. Its costs include staff wages, salaries and pensions, advertising and promotion costs, equipment and property maintenance costs, energy supply costs (such as the electricity to power the machines that make the products), and raw materials costs. It must pay back whatever it has borrowed. It must also pay a significant amount of money to the government in tax.

Cash flow

Cash flow is the rate at which money enters and leaves a business. When a company sells its products, it must make sure it is paid as soon as possible; otherwise it might not be able to pay its own debts and bills on time. Many businesses fail because of cash flow difficulties that arise when they do not have enough money to pay a debt or bill.

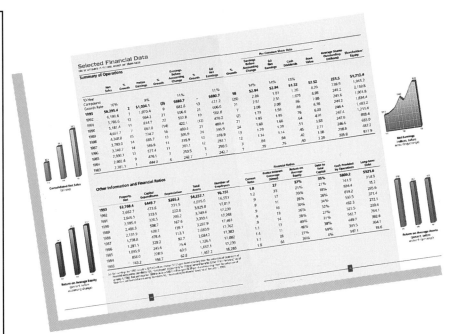

Profit and loss

If during a year's trading the amount of a company's revenue from selling its goods and services is greater than the amount of money it pays out in costs (its expenses), then the company has made a profit. The company cannot keep all of this profit, called the gross profit or pre-tax profit. It has to pay a

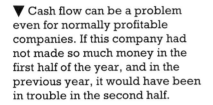

▼ Cash flow can be a problem even for normally profitable companies. If this company had not made so much money in the first half of the year, and in the previous year, it would have been in trouble in the second half.

BUSINESS MATTERS: KEEPING ACCOUNT

Companies need to know exactly what they have earned and spent in connection with their business and to predict what they are likely to earn and spend in the future. Every year, all public companies issue annual reports to let their stockholders know how they are doing. These reports include a summary of the company accounts. There are different types of account. A balance sheet describes the company's position at a certain time—for example, at the end of the month or year. It lists the company's assets—its property, earnings, and the money owed to it by customers and debtors—and its liabilities—the debts the company itself owes. A profit and loss account is a record of the year's trading.

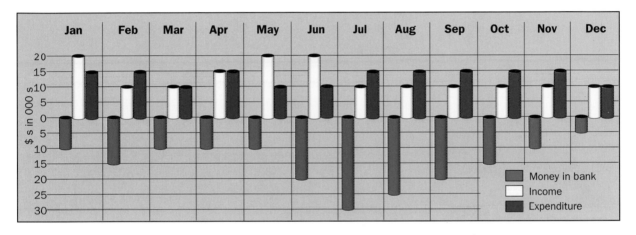

proportion of it to the government in tax. It also has to use some of it to repay long-term debts. If there is any left over, it is called a net profit. If a company's revenue is less than its expenses, it makes a pre-tax loss. If a company has made a small profit but is committed to repaying debts at a certain time, it could finish up the year making a net loss.

◄ Pages from a Kellogg company report. The figures in a company report tell stockholders and would-be investors how well the company is doing.

Investment

Many private companies have investors who own a share of the company. Public companies such as Kellogg trade their shares on the stock exchange. If a company wants to expand by developing a new product or buying another company, it will need more money. It may raise this by borrowing or issuing more shares. Some companies also make extra money by investing surplus profits in other companies. This is often how staff retirement funds are financed.

Kellogg's ®

The name on the box

Wherever you go in the world, you can recognize a box of *Kellogg's Corn Flakes* or any other Kellogg product. Even if the rest of the information on the box is in Japanese or Greek, the color and style of the name *Kellogg's* stays the same. This is Kellogg Company's logo (short for logogram), the distinctive symbol in red flowing script, by which its products are known around the world. Many companies attach great importance to their logos. A successful logo helps to register a company's

BUSINESS MATTERS: PATENTS AND TRADEMARKS

In May 1894, J.H. Kellogg took out a patent on the new flaked wheat, named Granose, and extended it to cover oats, barley, corn and other grains. A patent is an official government grant (or right) given to an inventor that no one else may use his invention without seeking permission and paying a fee called a royalty. A trademark is a word or phrase, picture, sound or symbol that distinguishes one company's

TM

◀ All Kellogg's characters are protected by trademarks. The perky *Toucan Sam* appears on *Froot Loops*. The frog opposite "digs" *Smacks*.

products from those of another. Logos are typical trademarks, and so are brand names (*Rice Krispies*, *Frosties*, etc), and images on packaging, such as the rooster on a box of *Kellogg's Corn Flakes*. Companies may register the trademarks they own to give them legal protection and stop anybody else from using them. Because patents and trademarks represent a company's unique skill and reputation, they have a financial value and are carefully guarded—and sometimes disputed. J.H. lost his sole right to manufacture flaked grain cereals in a court battle with W.K. in 1903.

A BOX TO READ

A typical *Kellogg's* box shows a large photograph of a bowl of cereal with or without a person or character enjoying it. The signature and name of the cereal are in bold letters at the top. The back and sides are covered with nutrition and other information, as well as an ever-changing selection of things to read and do, chosen to suit the typical consumer, games for the children, interesting information and offers for adults. There is always lots to read on a Kellogg box.

image in people's minds. Customers instantly recognize the symbol and know that the product it represents is one that they can trust.

The *Kellogg's* logo goes right back to 1903. It was adapted from W.K.'s signature and has changed remarkably little over the years. The reason for signing the boxes was a practical one. As soon as its products began to be popular, the company became the victim of imitators. Competition was fierce and W.K. was determined to protect his invention and not let others capitalize on it.

Putting on the style

As well as putting a stamp of genuineness on the boxes, the *Kellogg's* logo looks important and attractive. It helps to make the product stand out from other similar products on the supermarket shelves. But it is only one part of the *Kellogg's* image. All *Kellogg's* boxes and advertisements are designed to look bright and interesting. They have a consistent "look" which is continuously changing to keep up with the times and with new products, but nevertheless maintains the unmistakable Kellogg's style.

TM

Competition

Kellogg claims 42 percent of the world market in breakfast cereals. Out of the bewildering number of breakfast foods available, a large number, including many famous names such as *Grape Nuts*, *Quaker Oats*, and *Shredded Wheat*, are made by firms other than Kellogg. But, of the 15 top-selling brands of cereal on sale world-wide, 12 are manufactured by Kellogg. To keep its market share and stay ahead of its competitors, it is vital for Kellogg to create new products.

Competitors at home

Kellogg's largest competitor in the United States is General Mills Inc. It came into existence in 1928, taking over a long-established flour-milling company in the process, and during the Great Depression of the 1930s established itself in the cereals and flour markets. Its most popular brands in the United States have been *Wheaties*, *Cheerios*, *Cocoa Puffs*, and

▲ *Cheerios* is the biggest brand belonging to General Mills. The company's products are marketed outside North America by a joint venture with Nestlé called Cereal Partners Worldwide (CPW).

▼ *Shredded Wheat* was invented before *Corn Flakes* and has never lost its popularity. John Kellogg began his search for a comparable health food in response to it.

Lucky Charms. In 1996 it acquired *Chex* and other branded products from Ralston Foods, a company that was established in St. Louis in 1894 as the Ralston Purina Company. It originally marketed animal feed but later produced whole wheat cereals.

Other competitors in the United States include Quaker Oats of Chicago, famous for its porridge but also for familiar cold ready-to-eat cereals such as *Sugar Puffs*, with its advertising campaigns featuring the famous Honey Monster.

Like other brand-owners, Kellogg also faces competition from supermarket own-brands, which mimic the contents and packaging of its products. Fortunately for Kellogg, its logo and packaging are so distinctive that it is difficult for imitators to produce look-alike products that could be sold legally.

▲ Oatmeal has to be cooked but that has not lessened the popularity of *Quaker Oats*. *Sugar Puffs* are eaten cold but are a hot favorite with children.

Competitors abroad

Kellogg's global competitors include Cereal Partners World-wide, a joint venture between General Mills and Nestlé, the huge multinational food company based in Switzerland. Among its best-known cereal products are *Shredded Wheat*, a cereal even older than *Kellogg's Corn Flakes*, and *Clusters*, a nut-based cereal. Weetabix Ltd is the leading British cereal manufacturer. It makes brand-leaders *Weetabix*, *Ready Brek*, *Alpen* and many other cereals.

BUSINESS MATTERS: FREE-ENTERPRISE AND COMPETITION

Competition in business is the fight for customers and profits between two or more enterprises in the same field. People who believe in a market free of government regulations or any other form of control support competition. They claim it forces up standards as firms try to outdo each other in product quality and business efficiency. It also keeps prices down. Without competition businesses can charge what they like. But with competition, rival firms seek to attract customers by charging lower prices than their competitors.

BUSINESS MATTERS: OWN BRANDS

Because of their buying power, supermarket chains have become strong competitors to brand-owners. They stock all the major brands on their shelves so that customers can find their favorites. But, alongside them, they stock their own virtually identical products—at a lower price. Ralston Foods is the largest producer of own-brand cereals in the United States. Often, but never in Kellogg's case, the own-brand products are produced for the supermarket by the neighboring brand-owner. The names and packets are different but the contents are the same. In these cases the brand-owner simply makes a reduced profit on the goods. Where the goods are supplied by rival, but less well-known, companies, the brand-owner may lose out. That is why it is so important that a company like Kellogg has a brand with a unique appearance that can be relied upon for quality— and defended in court.

▲ As well as its own popular brands, Weetabix makes many own-brand cereals for supermarkets in the UK.

Kellogg's public face

The marketing and design staff, the promotions people, and the advertising agencies Kellogg uses all work together to create a good impression of the company and its products in the consumer's mind. Paid television commercials and magazine ads help to attract and keep customers and give the company a positive image with the public. Free publicity in the form of stories that reflect well on the company are also important in promoting the company's image. Like all big companies, Kellogg keeps the press up-to-date with company achievements and seeks good publicity at local and national levels. When it has a story, such as being the first company to market ready-to-eat cereals in India, it can guarantee good coverage in the press.

▲ A boy scout devouring his *Corn Flakes* was the perfect symbol of youthful health to enhance Kellogg's image in its early days.

▶ The emblem on the door of this delivery truck is good publicity. It is the "Royal Warrant," which is awarded to companies that suppy products to members of the British royal family.

BUSINESS MATTERS: PUBLICITY

Publicity is not paid for directly by companies, although most firms put a lot of effort into trying to get good publicity. A favorable article can generate more business than an expensive advertisement. Bad publicity keeps a company's image in people's minds but it may be harmful. If a food company's product accidentally poisoned somebody, media coverage could be very damaging. So all big companies make an effort to combat misleading or adverse stories.

Famous faces

A large company such as Kellogg is of such local and national importance that it is influential enough to invite visiting dignitaries—from princes to presidents—to its premises. Pictures of the visits afford perfect picture opportunities for the press. But Kellogg does not rely on glamour. It sees itself as part of the community where it operates. Rather than inviting a celebrity to open a major new plant in Britain, it invited the winner of a nationwide competition to do the honors, and an ordinary member of the public took center stage at this important and well-publicized event.

THE HEALTH MESSAGE

Everyone values their health. Busy parents are especially eager to give their children a good start to the day. Many of the ads devised for Kellogg emphasize the nutritional value of cereal. Magazine and newspaper ads of the early 1950s were more like illustrated educational features explaining the dietary value of breakfast. A television commercial of the 1970s emphasized the vitamins and iron in *Corn Flakes* through the medium of a song: "It's smart to start with *Kellogg's Corn Flakes*!" Today's ads may be more subtle, but the goal is the same—to keep people buying Kellogg's products.

▶ You may need a magnifying glass to read all Kellogg's claims for *All-Bran* in this ad. As ever, Kellogg was telling the truth at a time when many advertisers got away with making bogus claims about products.

◀ Kellogg has always made sure that its products appeal to all the family, young and old alike. Brands such as *Special K* are deliberately targeted at health-conscious adults.

▼ Today few parents would want to see their babies stuffed, but good food was not always as cheap or as plentiful as it is now.

CATCHING YOUNG CONSUMERS

From an early stage, Kellogg's advertising was geared to children. The Times Square sign featured a child saying "I want Kellogg's." Many ads are still aimed at children, especially those for *Coco Pops*, *Honey Smacks* and other pre-sweetened cereals. The friendly characters that go with each product have instant child-appeal. One series of ads directed at adults appealed to their nostalgia for the tastes of childhood with the slogan "Have you forgotten how good they are?"

Kellogg in the community

Companies are like individuals. They want to be liked and so they take good care of their image—that is, the way the public sees them. Kellogg knows the value of good public relations as well as good publicity. It has an image not only as an international company but also as a local one.

In each of the countries in which it operates, Kellogg has forged links with the local community. Its workers and their families feel themselves members of a larger family. Kellogg encourages its employees to take part in community projects. Locally and nationally, it seeks to sponsor organizations, sports events and projects that benefit the community. Kellogg also pledges itself to run its business in a way that is environmentally friendly. Where possible its packaging is recyclable.

▼ Kellogg provides schools and health organizations with a wealth of material that helps children and adults learn how to lead healthy lives and makes them familiar with the Kellogg name.

THE W.K. KELLOGG FOUNDATION

In 1930, W.K. used some of the great personal wealth he had earned to found a charitable organization called the W.K. Kellogg Foundation. The Foundation is and always has been an independent organization separate from Kellogg Company, but it holds stock in Kellogg Company and is represented on the board of directors. Set up for the welfare of children and to help people help themselves, the Kellogg Foundation today funds projects in health education, agriculture, leadership, and youth.

▲ W.K. and his dog stand before the door of the original W.K. Kellogg Foundation.

▶ Over the years the Kellogg Foundation has grown considerably and benefited many good causes. Thanks to W.K., the citizens of Battle Creek also have a community college and bird sanctuary that bear his name.

"I'll invest my money in people."
W.K. Kellogg

A biographical sketch of the Founder of
The Kellogg Company and
The W. K. Kellogg Foundation

▲ W.K.'s investment in people has helped thousands of individuals to better themselves and their circumstances.

Health education
One of the greatest services that Kellogg sees itself performing for the general public is in health information and education. Long before healthy eating became popular, Kellogg was busy informing the public about the importance of breakfast in a balanced diet. As early as the 1940s it devised special games for teachers to use when explaining about nutrition to younger children. Half a century later, it is still providing award-winning educational materials, now in the form of computer programs and health and fitness videos.

Using the profits
Kellogg's involvement in community and education projects allows it to use up some of its profits by giving them away in the form of charitable donations. In addition to Kellogg's genuine humanitarian motives, there is a sound business reason for making some charitable donations. They use money that might otherwise have to be paid in tax.

Tomorrow's Kellogg

▲ Kellogg is determined to wrap itself around the whole world. A billion people are targeted as future consumers.

No company can afford to stand still. Even a successful global organization such as Kellogg Company must change to keep up with changing technology and reduce its costs by becoming more efficient. It must keep on growing, expanding into new markets and increasing profits for its stockholders. The stated aim of Arnold G. Langbo is for the company to reach a billion new consumers.

New products

As well as selling ever more of its successful brands, the company will create more new products. To catch the attention of new consumers, especially children and people with non-western tastes, it will research appealing new flavors. In

► People in developed countries are increasingly eager to make healthy food choices but they constantly want new tastes. Kellogg offers both. *Basmati Flakes* are designed to appeal to Asian customers. Basmati is regarded as the best kind of rice.

the mid-1990s, Kellogg has already begun making a flaked cereal based on basmati rice and a new cereal for the United States market called *Kellogg's Temptations*. With the purchase of Lender's Bagel Bakery, it has expanded into bakery products.

As people become more and more concerned about eating more healthfully, the company will make ever greater efforts to provide consumers with healthy breakfasts. It will fortify its cereals with vitamins and minerals and provide low-fat, high-fiber products, in line with the latest medical recommendations.

◀ Asian children are as fond as western children of *Tony the Tiger* and the taste of *Frosties*. Kellogg is introducing its most popular brands to Asia with new brands devised to suit local tastes.

New places

Kellogg will expand the developing North American convenience foods business into other countries and continue to open up new markets for its core products. Eastern Europe and Asia are huge markets with vast populations gradually acquiring enough money to purchase western goods and adopt western eating habits. In 1993, Kellogg opened the first cereal-food plant in Eastern Europe. Its new plant in Riga, Latvia, will serve a young market in a region where cheese and meat, not cereal, form the traditional breakfast. Kellogg opened its first plant in India in 1994, its first in China in 1995 and one in Thailand in 1997.

INVESTING FOR THE FUTURE

After investing its profits in production and sales, or using them for charitable purposes, Kellogg invests any surplus to make more profits for its stockholders. Whenever share prices in general are low Kellogg buys its own stock. This builds the capital of the company, increases the company's own control over its future, and enables it to pay its individual stockholders more.

◀ Wherever people go, Kellogg will seek to go, ever ready to sell its nutritious, tasty cereals.

Red letter days ahead

Kellogg's stockholders, employees and consumers know that whatever Kellogg does to attract new consumers and beat competitors, certain things will never change. Kellogg's will always use the best ingredients, blend and cook them to the highest standard, pay strict attention to healthy nutrition, and proclaim its name in big red letters.

Create your own business

◀ Make sure people know about your magazine. Keep the articles and jokes in it secret but make sure that everyone is dying to read them.

Kellogg has been in business for nearly a hundred years. Its success is founded on the quality of its product, the simplicity of its business and the creativity of its advertising. See if you can create a profitable business.

Product
Think of a good idea for a product that you can make, advertise and sell simply. You could produce a magazine and use a promotional gimmick to sell it. Find talented people to write articles, draw cartoons and write or collect jokes. Think of a contest, such as a quiz or puzzle to be solved. Don't make it too easy or too

difficult. If you want only one winner, you may need to invent a tiebreaker. Ask your school and parents for permission before you go ahead. If they approve, make a mock-up of one issue of the magazine.

Sponsorship
You will need a really good prize for your contest. Find a local company which will give you the prize in exchange for publicity. Show the company the mock-up and explain how you will publicize their product.

Research
Find out who your customers will be, what they would like

to see in the magazine and how much they would be prepared to pay for it.

People
Select or elect a small team to produce the magazine and sell it. You will need writers, artists and designers, people to publicize, sell and distribute the copies and somebody to take care of the money.

Capital
You will need some money to start with. If everyone contributes some of their own money they will find their parents willing to lend some. You must offer to return their money with interest.

CAPITAL

PEOPLE

EQUIPMENT

MARKETING

◀ Plan your business carefully. Remember you need capital, people, equipment and marketing.

▼ Real businesses present their figures as a profit and loss account like this.

PROFIT AND LOSS ACCOUNT		
Sales		400.00
Less Cost of Sales		
Paper	90.00	
Pictures	50.00	
Disks	10.00	
Poster	20.00	
	170.00	(170.00)
Gross profit		230.00
Less Overhead		
Wages	10.00	
Stationery	5.00	
Telephone	5.00	
Fares	4.00	
	24.00	(24.00)
Net profit		206.00
Loan repayment	150.00	
Interest	7.50	
	157.50	(157.50)
Net profit after interest		72.50

Planning

Work out how to produce the magazine: who and what you need and how long each stage will take and cost. Estimate how many copies you can sell. What is the maximum number? What is the minimum? What is the likely number?

Costing

Before you start, see if your project will work financially. How much will the paper for the magazine cost? How much will the computer disks cost? How much will it cost to make posters? Remember your overhead—the cost of phone calls, stationery, postage and bus fares.

Work out the cost per item by adding all the costs together and dividing them by the number of copies you plan to print.

Publicity

While the magazine is in production, drum up publicity. Tell people about the contest and the sponsor. Put up posters in school, in stores, in the library and elsewhere. Ask the local paper to run a story.

Selling

Get everyone on the team selling on the days you publish. Get customers to buy more than one copy so that they can have more than

one attempt at the contest.

Accounts

Keep accurate records of all the money you spend and receive. Repay your investors and decide what to do with the rest of the profit. Will you give it to a charitable organization? Will you use it to make future issues better or to make another magazine entirely? Perhaps you will think of a giveaway item next time round to promote sales.

The language of business

Accountant Person who keeps or inspects accounts. See also Treasurer.

Advertising Making publicly known. Advertisers use television, radio, newspapers and so on to tell everyone how good their product is. See also Promotion.

Aerobics Vigorous exercise that aims to enrich the blood with oxygen and strengthen the heart.

Analyze To examine minutely.

Assets Anything owned by a business, including property, money, goods and machines.

Bagel Hard, ring-shaped bread roll.

Bankrupt Having no money in the bank or any means of paying debts.

Billion A thousand million.

Board of directors See Directors.

Bookkeeper Person who keeps a continuous record of a company's financial transactions.

Boom A time when business is good and customers can afford to buy products.

Bran The fibrous husks of various grains, separated from the flour during milling.

Brand The name of a company's product. See also Trademark.

Business An organization that sells goods or services.

Caffeine A stimulant found in coffee, tea and cola.

Calorie A measure of the energy value of food.

Capital Money needed to start a business and keep it going.

Carbohydrate Starch and sugars.

Caramelize To color brown by heating sugar.

Cash flow The rate at which money enters and leaves a business during any period of time.

Cereal Any grass that produces an edible grain, such as barley, corn, oats, rice and rye.

Chairman The person who heads a committee or board of directors. Also called a chairperson or chair.

Chief executive The highest-ranking officer in a company who has full power to act and make decisions on behalf of the company.

Commercial To do with trade.

Company Organization of a group of people to carry on a business. Companies may be small or large, public or private.

Company secretary A person who records the meetings and decisions of the board of directors.

Competition The struggle for customers and profits between two or more enterprises in the same field.

Consignment A collection of goods shipped or transported at one time. See Shipper.

Consumer The final purchaser or user of an article. See also Customer.

Convenience food A food that needs little or no preparation and is ready to eat at any time.

Conveyer belt A continuously moving belt that transports goods, materials or packages during manufacture.

Corporate officers Senior managers of a corporation. They include the chief executive officer, the president, the executive officers and vice-presidents. See Directors.

Costs The amount of capital that it takes to make or sell a product or service.

Credit To give credit is to allow time for a payment to be made.

Croissant A flaky pastry roll made in the shape of a crescent.

Customer Anyone who buys from a seller, especially one who buys regularly. See also Retailer.

Directors People who guide the activities of a company and make its most important decisions. They are members of the board of directors, which is led by the chairman or chief executive. The directors report to a managing director, who may also be the chairman of the board. See also Corporate officers.

Distribution The means by which a product gets from a manufacturer to a customer.

Diversification The widening of the range of goods and services.

Dividend A small part of a company's profits paid to shareholders.

Earnings Money gained by a person working or a company selling.

Employee A person who works for an employer (another person or a company) in return for pay.

Entrepreneur An enterprising business person who is willing to take risks.

Ethical In accordance with moral principles and professional standards.

Executive director A director who works for a company. A non-executive director is a member of the board but is not employed by the company. See also Directors.

Fiber Substance in vegetable foods that contains no nutrients but aids digestion.

Financial director Chief financial officer responsible for financial planning, making and receiving payments and keeping records.

Financial To do with money.

Firm Another word for a business or company.

Focus group Specially selected discussion groups who assess products and make suggestions.

Folic acid B-group vitamin, deficiency of which causes anemia and birth defects.

Food technologist An expert in the content, energy value and nutritional value of food.

Fortify To make foods more nutritious by the addition of extra vitamins or minerals.

Free enterprise System that allows businesses to operate in a market free from state control or interference and customs duties.

General council Director who supervises all the legal aspects of a company's business.

Globalize To make international.

Goods Things other than food produced by a business.

Grain Fruit of a cereal plant, consisting of a kernel surrounded by a protective husk.

Grits Edible part of the corn used for making Corn Flakes.

Gross See Net and gross.

Growth Expansion of a business to increase profits.

Human resources The people who work for a business. Also called staff or personnel.

Image How a company is seen by the public.

Income The money that a business or individual receives from earnings or investments.

Insurance The business of providing financial protection for life, health and property in return for regular payments called premiums.

Interest Money paid to banks or investors for use of the money they have lent.

Invest To put money into a business or buy shares in it.

Kernel A grain of wheat or other cereal.

Labor Collective name for workers, especially manual workers.

Logo Short for logogram. A sign or symbol that represents a word and is often used as a trademark.

Loss The money that a business loses when it spends more than it earns.

Maize Cereal plant known also as corn on the cob, or simply as corn.

Malt Sweet, tasty substance made by steeping cereal grains in water, and allowing them to sprout and dry.

Manager A person who controls or organizes a business or part of it and organizes staff.

Manufacturer A business that makes or produces goods.

Market research Surveying people's tastes and requirements to assess the demand for a product.

Market The total number of buyers and sellers of a product.

Marketing All the activities involved in putting a product on the market, including research and development, distribution and sales, pricing and promotion.

Mass market The majority of the population. Mostly low-priced products sell to the mass market.

Media Newspapers, television, and radio considered collectively.

Minerals Substances in food, such as calcium, magnesium, and phosphorus, that help build body tissues and are vital for health.

Muesli A breakfast food originating in Switzerland and consisting of rolled oats, nuts, and fruit eaten with milk or yogurt.

Net and gross A gross amount is money paid or earned before tax and other contributions have been deducted to leave a net amount.

Non-executive director See Executive director.

Non-profit Not run to make a profit for itself. Many charities and voluntary organizations are non-profit.

Nutrition The science of food and its use by the body.

Oats Cereal used in such breakfast foods as granola and oatmeal.

Overheads General costs, such as rent, heating, stationery and so on, that do not relate to a specific operation or item.

Own brand Goods manufactured on behalf of a supermarket and sold under the supermarket's name.

Patent An official government document that establishes an individual's or company's exclusive right or title to an invention for a certain period.

Physical resources Things such as buildings, machines and raw materials that a business uses.

Plant Factory or machinery used in a factory.

Porridge A breakfast food made from oatmeal and cooked in water or milk until it thickens.

Premium 1 A regular payment to an insurance company. 2 Small item given away with goods to encourage purchase.

Private company A company that is owned by an individual or group of individuals, and whose shares are not traded on the stock exchange. See also Public company.

Product The thing that a business sells. Products can be goods or services.

Profit The difference between what a company earns and its costs.

Promotion 1 Moving up the employment scale to a better job. 2 Encouraging sales by advertising, publicity and other incentives such as giveaways.

Protein Substances in foods, such as meat, milk, eggs, grains, nuts and peas, that are essential for the growth, health and repair of the body.

Public company A business that offers shares of itself for sale to the general public.

Publicity News or information about a company's activities and products.

Quality control The series of checks that a company makes to ensure that its products meet legal and internal standards of quality and safety.

Raw materials The ingredients needed to make a product.

Recession A time of unfavorable economic conditions when demand for products is low.

Recyclable Able to be re-used.

Research and development Investigation into new developments in design, technology and other fields and the creation of trial products.

Retailer Business such as a shop or supermarket that sells goods in small numbers to the public. Retailers generally buy their goods from wholesalers who buy in bulk from manufacturers.

Rotary ovens Ovens in which fans distribute the heated air evenly to ensure even roasting.

Salary Money paid in fixed amounts, usually monthly, to non-manual or office workers.

Sanitarium Place for the treatment of invalids and people convalescing. Usually spelt sanatorium in Britain.

Senior vice-president See Corporate officers.

Shareholder A person who owns shares in a company. Also called a stockholder.

Shares Tiny portions of a company's capital value. The price at which shares are bought and sold goes up and down according to the company's success. See also Stock.

Shipper A person or company who sends cases of goods to retailers by road, rail or sea.

Slogan A spoken or written phrase used on packaging and in advertisements to help fix a product in the public mind.

Sponsor Person or company who provides money or other assistance for sporting, charitable or cultural events.

Staff All the people who work for a company, or all the workers below management level.

Stakeholder Someone who has a stake or financial interest in a business or enterprise.

State control Regulation of industry and other areas by the government. See Free enterprise.

Stock 1 Products stored ready for sale by a company. 2 A block of shares.

Stock exchange See Stock market.

Stock market Exchange where stocks and shares are bought and sold.

Stockholder A person who holds stock. A shareholder.

Subsidiary A business partly or wholly owned by another business.

Surplus More than is needed.

Target market A specific group of potential customers.

Tax Money that businesses and individuals have to pay the government from their earnings.

Technology The application of science to industry.

Temper To bring to a certain consistency.

Trade union An association formed by workers to improve their pay and working conditions.

Trademark A name, design, symbol or some distinguishing mark that makes a company or product unique and recognizable.

Treasurer Another name for the financial director or chief accountant of a company. See Corporate officers; Directors.

Unemployment Shortage of paid work. Levels of unemployment are high during a recession.

Vice-president Person responsible to a senior vice-president or to the board of directors for work done by people under his or her supervision.

Vitamin Chemicals found in foods or added to them that the body needs to function properly.

Waffles A crisp golden batter cake made with a waffle iron.

Wage Weekly payment made on the basis of an hourly rate to manual workers.

Wheat Cereal used for making bread, pasta and high-fiber cereals. Also known as corn in Britain.

Wholesaler See Retailer.

Index

Numbers in *italics* indicate pictures and diagrams; those in **bold** indicate panel references.